READING CHAMPION

The Lost Bear

by **Jackie Walter** and **Pat Corrigan**

W

Dad took Jem to the park.

Jem took Bear.

"I want to go on the swings,"
said Jem.

Jem got to the swings.

He looked for Bear.

He could not see him.

Dad and Jem went back
to the gate to look for Bear.
But Bear was not there.

"Come on, Dad," said Jem.
"We must look for him."

Bear was playing on the swings.

He was having fun.

Dad and Jem went back
to look for Bear by the swings.
But Bear was not there.

"Where is he?" said Jem.

Bear was playing

on the roundabout.

"Hold on, Bear," shouted the boy.

Dad and Jem went to look
for Bear by the roundabout.
But Bear was not there.

"Oh no!" said Jem.
"Bear is lost!"

Bear was playing on the slide.

Down, down, down he went.

Dad and Jem went to look
for Bear by the slide.
But Bear was not there.
Jem was sad.

Bear was playing in the sandpit.

He was digging a hole.

Jem went up to the top of the slide.
He looked up and down the park.

"I can see Bear," shouted Jem.
"Stop!"

"Stop!" shouted the boy.

Jem and Dad ran after Bear.

The boy ran after Bear.

"He is not your bear," said Jem.

"He is my bear and I love him."

The boy looked at Jem.

"He is your bear," he said.
"Here you are."

"Thank you," said Jem.

He was happy to have Bear back.

He looked at the boy.

"Come on," he said.

"Let's go on the see-saw."

Bear was happy too.

He had two friends.

Story trail

Start

Start at the beginning of the story trail. Ask your child to retell the story in their own words, pointing to each picture in turn to recall the sequence of events.

Independent Reading

This series is designed to provide an opportunity for your child to read on their own. These notes are written for you to help your child choose a book and to read it independently.

In school, your child's teacher will often be using reading books which have been banded to support the process of learning to read. Use the book band colour your child is reading in school to help you make a good choice. *The Lost Bear* is a good choice for children reading at Blue Band in their classroom to read independently.

The aim of independent reading is to read this book with ease, so that your child enjoys the story and relates it to their own experiences.

About the book

Jem loves to take Bear wherever he goes. But one day, at the park, he loses Bear. Dad and Jem search everywhere but Bear is busy having an adventure all of his own.

Before reading

Help your child to learn how to make good choices by asking: "Why did you choose this book? Why do you think you will enjoy it?" Look at the cover together and ask: "What do you think the story will be about?" Support your child to think of what they already know about the story context. Read the title aloud and ask: "What do you think happens to Bear?" Remind your child that they can try to sound out the letters to make a word if they get stuck.

Decide together whether your child will read the story independently or read it aloud to you. When books are short, as at Blue Band, your child may wish to do both!

During reading

If reading aloud, support your child if they hesitate or ask for help by telling the word. Remind your child of what they know and what they can do independently.

If reading to themselves, remind your child that they can come and ask for your help if stuck.

After reading

Support comprehension by asking your child to tell you about the story. Use the story trail to encourage your child to retell the story in the right sequence, in their own words.

Give your child a chance to respond to the story: "Did you have a favourite part? How do you think Jem felt when he lost Bear? How do you think the other boy felt when Jem found Bear?" Help your child think about the messages in the book that go beyond the story and ask: "Why do you think the boy gives Jem his bear back? Why are both boys happy in the end?"

Extending learning

Help your child understand the story structure by using the same sentence patterns and adding some new elements. "Let's make up a new story. 'Dad took Ben to the supermarket. Ben took Tiger. "I want to look at the popcorn," said Ben. They got to the car. Ben looked for Tiger. He could not see it.' What will happen in your story?" In the classroom your child's teacher may be reinforcing punctuation. On a few of the pages, check your child can recognise capital letters, full stops, exclamation marks and question marks by asking them to point these out.

Franklin Watts
First published in Great Britain in 2019
by The Watts Publishing Group

Copyright © The Watts Publishing Group 2019

Series Editors: Jackie Hamley and Melanie Palmer
Series Advisors: Dr Sue Bodman and Glen Franklin
Series Designer: Peter Scoulding

A CIP catalogue record for this book is
available from the British Library.

ISBN 978 1 4451 6810 4 (hbk)
ISBN 978 1 4451 6812 8 (pbk)
ISBN 978 1 4451 6811 1 (library ebook)

Printed in China

Franklin Watts
An imprint of
Hachette Children's Group
Part of The Watts Publishing Group
Carmelite House
50 Victoria Embankment
London EC4Y 0DZ

An Hachette UK Company
www.hachette.co.uk

www.franklinwatts.co.uk